Mummies Around the World

Emma Carlson-Berne

Lerner Publications • Minneapolis

Copyright © 2024 by Lerner Publishing Group, Inc.

All rights reserved. International copyright secured. No part of this book may be reproduced, stored in a retrieval system, or transmitted in any form or by any means—electronic, mechanical, photocopying, recording, or otherwise—without the prior written permission of Lerner Publishing Group, Inc., except for the inclusion of brief quotations in an acknowledged review.

Lerner Publications Company
An imprint of Lerner Publishing Group, Inc.
241 First Avenue North
Minneapolis, MN 55401 USA

For reading levels and more information, look up this title at www.lernerbooks.com.

Main body text set in Billy Infant Regular. Typeface provided by SparkType.

Library of Congress Cataloging-in-Publication Data

Names: Berne, Emma Carlson, 1979- author.
Title: Mummies around the world / Emma Carlson Berne.
Description: Minneapolis, MN: Lerner Publications, [2023] | Series: Lightning Bolt Books — That's scary! | Includes bibliographical references and index. | Audience: Ages 6-9 years | Audience: Grades 2-3 | Summary: "From Egyptian pharaohs to bodies trapped in bogs, young readers will learn about human and animal mummies throughout history. This book explores how mummies are made and the spooky stories around them"—Provided by publisher.
Identifiers: LCCN 2022046116 (print) | LCCN 2022046117 (ebook) | ISBN 9781728491196 (Library Binding) | ISBN 9798765603338 (Paperback) | ISBN 9781728498744 (eBook)
Subjects: LCSH: Mummies—Juvenile literature.
Classification: LCC GN293 .B468 2023 (print) | LCC GN293 (ebook) | DDC 393/.3—dc23/eng/20221201

LC record available at https://lccn.loc.gov/2022046116
LC ebook record available at https://lccn.loc.gov/2022046117

Manufactured in the United States of America
1-53050-51068-1/17/2023

Table of Contents

Meeting a Mummy — 4

Egyptian Mummies — 6

Bog People — 10

The Mummies of the Chinchorro — 14

Fun Facts — 20

Animal Mummies — 21

Glossary — 22

Learn More — 23

Index — 24

Meeting a Mummy

A human figure lies on a table. It is wrapped in strips of cloth. The person inside has been dead for thousands of years. **It's a mummy!**

Mummies are found all around the globe.

Mummies are dead, but sometimes they almost look as if they are alive. Some people imagine that a mummy will put a curse on anyone who disturbs its coffin.

Egyptian Mummies

A mummy is a person or an animal whose body has been preserved after death. Their body does not rot because it has been dried or embalmed.

Ancient Egyptians also mummified animals, such as cats.

The ancient Egyptians mummified many of their dead people. The Egyptians believed that the body of a person was the home of the soul. By preserving the body, they were keeping the soul in its home.

The organs of Egyptian mummies were placed in containers called canopic jars.

To make a mummy, Egyptians first took out the stomach, brain, and other organs from the corpse. They covered the corpse with salt. The salt dried out the body.

Later, they wrapped the mummy in long strips of cloth. Then they put the mummy in a painted coffin called a sarcophagus.

Most sarcophagi are made out of stone.

Bog People

Sometimes, nature mummifies people and animals. In the bogs of Ireland, Denmark, and the Netherlands, people have found mummies buried in the ground.

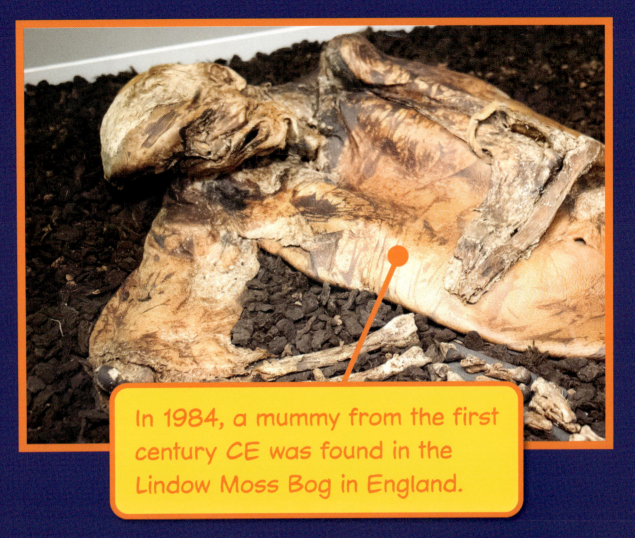

In 1984, a mummy from the first century CE was found in the Lindow Moss Bog in England.

Archaeologists have discovered mummified people in bogs who lived during prehistoric times. When the prehistoric people died, they were buried in the bogs.

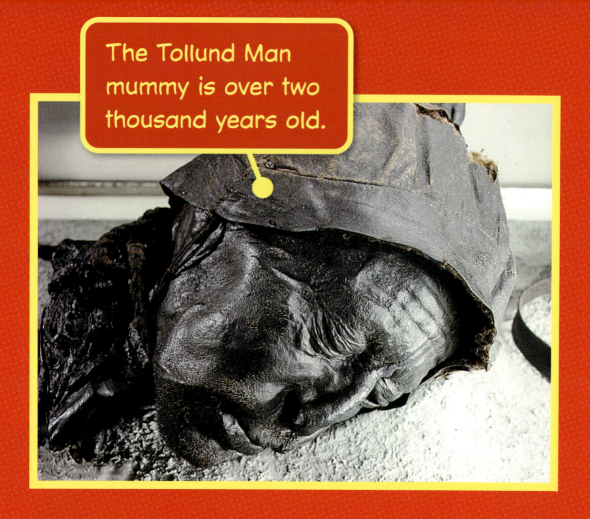

The Tollund Man mummy is over two thousand years old.

These mummies are not wrapped up like Egyptian mummies. These mummies are wearing the clothes they were buried in. The natural chemicals in the bog have preserved the bodies and the clothes on them.

Scientists can study the clothes to see if they came from faraway places. This helps historians learn more about how the people in this time and place traded with other people.

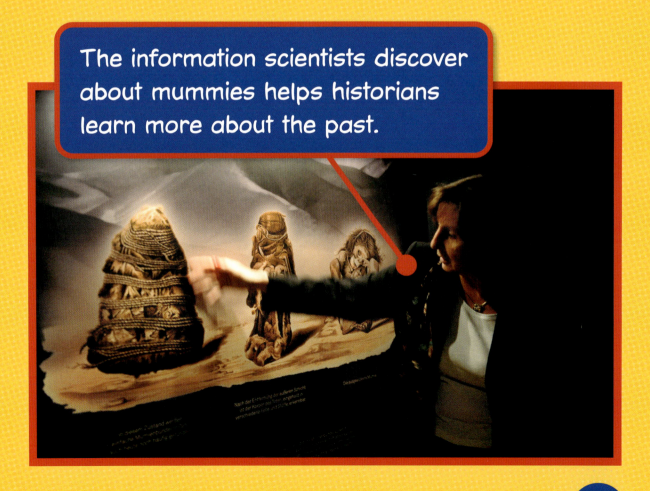

The information scientists discover about mummies helps historians learn more about the past.

The Mummies of the Chinchorro

The ancient Chinchorro people made mummies too. These people lived in Peru and Chile from about 7000 to 1500 BCE.

The oldest Chinchorro mummy is over seven thousand years old.

Like ancient Egyptians, the Chinchorro took out the corpse's organs. They dried the organs and peeled off the corpse's skin. They put hot coals inside the body to dry it.

A mummy on display in a museum in Chile

When the body was dry, they put sticks inside it to make it straight. They stuffed it full of grasses. Then they put the dried skin back on.

They made a clay mask for the mummy's face. They sewed on fake hair. Then the Chinchorro painted the mummy's body with black or red paint.

The clay masks of Chinchorro mummies have inspired a line of sculptures in Chile.

The Chinchorro buried their mummies in special graves. **People who live near the graves sometimes find the mummies by accident.**

A prehistoric Chinchorro site

The Chinchorro people were fishers who used harpoons and fishing hooks made of shells.

Scientists are studying the Chinchorro mummies to learn more about them. Mummies anywhere are special—and a little spooky!

Fun Facts

- Egyptians removed the organs from inside a mummy's body. They treated them so they would not rot and then placed them in special jars that were buried with the mummy.

- When scientists found a baby mammoth frozen in the earth in the Yukon in Canada in 2022, they estimated that she had died about thirty thousand years ago.

- Some bog mummies were murdered. A bog mummy discovered in Denmark in 1950 was strangled with a rope over 2000 years ago. The rope was still twisted around his neck.

Animal Mummies

Animals can be mummies too! People have discovered ancient animals frozen in the ground or in glaciers. In 2016, a miner in northern Canada found a frozen wolf puppy. Scientists think she died fifty-seven thousand years ago!

The ancient Egyptians mummified animals as well as people. Scientists have found mummies of birds, cats, bulls, and even snakes! These animals were dried and wrapped with cloth, just like human mummies.

Glossary

archaeologist: one who studies material remains of past human life and activities

bog: a type of wetland with spongy, wet ground

corpse: a dead body

embalm: to treat a dead body to preserve it from decay

preserve: to keep

sarcophagus: a coffin, often made of stone and painted

soul: the spiritual part of a person that some believe gives life to a body

Learn More

Britannica Kids: Mummy
https://kids.britannica.com/kids/article/mummy/351403

Faust, Daniel R. *Ancient Egypt*. New York: Gareth Stevens, 2019.

Murray, Julie. *Ötzi the Iceman*. Minneapolis: Dash!, 2022.

National Geographic Kids: How to Make a Mummy!
https://www.natgeokids.com/uk/discover/history/egypt/how-to-make-a-mummy/

O'Neill, Sean. *50 Things You Didn't Know about Ancient Egypt*. South Egremont, MA: Red Chair, 2020.

Peterson, Megan Cooley. *Bog Mummies: Where Did They Come From?* North Mankato, MN: Black Rabbit Books, 2019.

Index

ancient Egypt, 7–9
animals, 6, 10

bog, 10–12

Chinchorro, 14–15, 17–19
curse, 5

sarcophagus, 9

Photo Acknowledgments

Images used: Michele Burgess/Alamy Stock Photo, p. 4; Travel-Fr/Shutterstock.com, p. 5; Andrea Izzotti/Shutterstock.com, pp. 6, 7; savo1974/Shutterstock.com, p. 8; Ivan Soto Cobos/Shutterstock.com, p. 9; Westersoe/Getty Images, p. 10; Ian Thraves/Alamy Stock Photo, p. 11; Werner Forman/Getty Images, p. 12; Sueddeutsche Zeitung Photo/Alamy Stock Photo, p. 13; UDAZKENA/Alamy Stock Photo, pp. 14, 15, 18; Insights/Getty Images, p. 16; Sergio Donoso/EyeEm/Getty Images, p. 17; Jon G. Fuller/VWPics/Alamy Stock Photo, p. 19.
Cover: Andrea Izzotti/Shutterstock.com.